A·FIRST·BOOK·OF
WORDS

Illustrated by David Anstey
Written by A J Wood

MODERN PUBLISHING
A Division of Unisystems, Inc.
New York, New York 10022

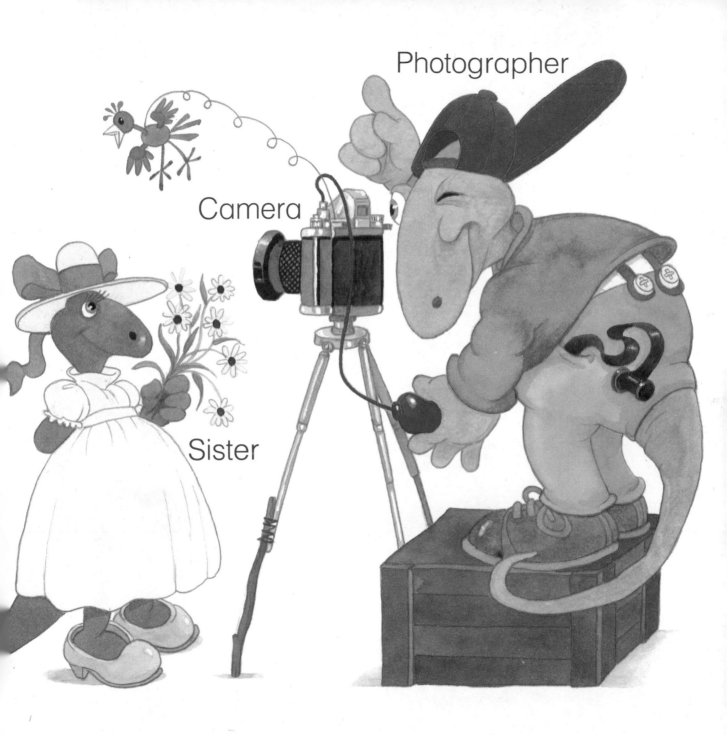

Photographer

Camera

Sister

House

Door

Neighbor

Path

Hedge

Gate

MEALTIME

Cup and saucer

Teapot

Spoon

Glass

Bowl

Knife

Plate

Fork

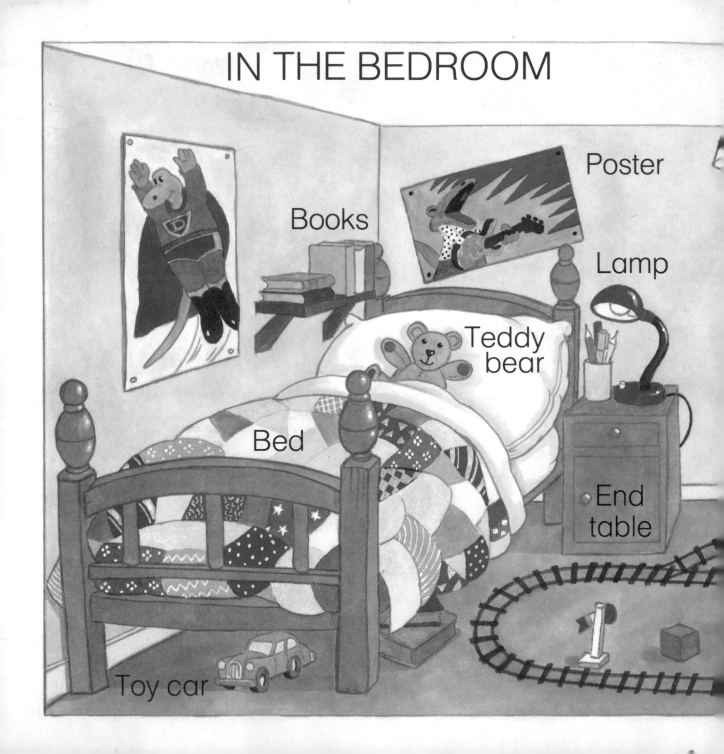

IN THE BEDROOM

Robe

Guitar

Window shade

Tennis racquet

Chair

Train

Blocks

Doll

Ball

Toy box

BATHTIME

Mirror

Toothbrush

Towel

Toothpaste

Sink

Boat

Shirt

Coat

Scarf

Socks

Jeans

Sneakers

AT THE PLAYGROUND

Swing

Seesaw

Shovel

Pail

Sandbox

Slide

Jump rope

Marbles

Bench

THE PETTING ZOO

Horse

Duck

Turtle

Donkey

Bird

Cow

Goat

Sheep

Rabbit Mouse

Rooster

OUT AND ABOUT

Train

Bus

Motorcycle

Boat

Skateboard

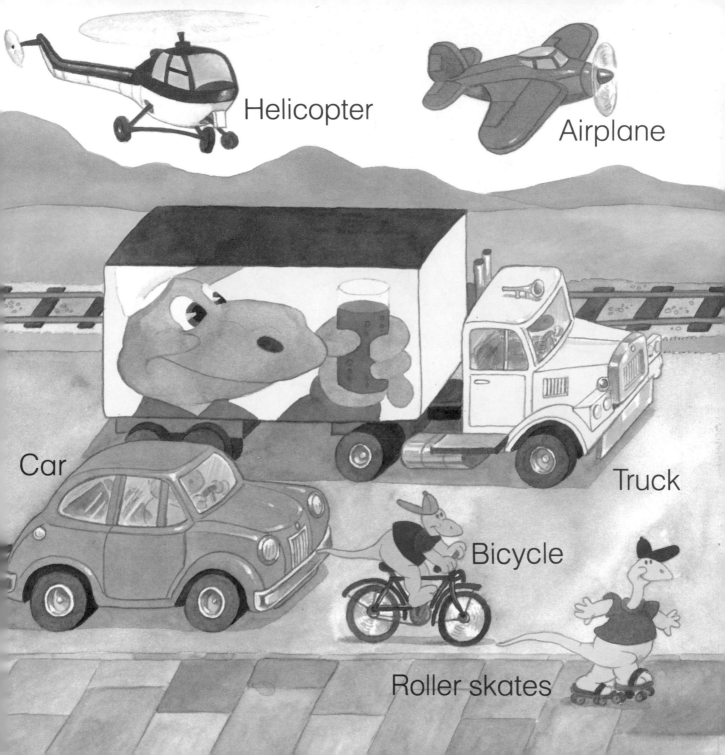

Helicopter

Airplane

Car

Truck

Bicycle

Roller skates

THINGS WE DO

Sing

Dance

Run

Walk

Jump

Eat

Drink

Wash

Laugh

Cry

Sleep

WORD QUIZ

Can you remember the names of these objects? You can find them all in the pages of this book. Point your finger at each one and say its name.

WORD LIST

Airplane

Baby
Bag
Ball
Bathtub
Bed
Bedroom
Bench
Bicycle
Bird
Blocks
Boat
Books
Bowl
Brother
Bubble bath
Bubbles
Bus
Bush

Camera
Car
Chair
Chimney
Coat
Cow
Cry
Cup

Daddy
Dance
Dinosaur
Dog
Doll
Donkey
Door
Dress
Drink
Duck

Eat
End table

Family
Faucet
Fish
Flowers
Fork

Garden
Gate
Glass
Goat
Grandma
Grandpa
Guitar

Hat

Hedge
Helicopter
Home
Horse
House

Jeans
Jump
Jump rope

Knife

Lamp
Laugh
Letter

Mailman
Marbles
Mirror
Mommy
Motorcycle
Mouse

Neighbor

Package
Pail
Path
Petting zoo

Photographer
Plate
Playground
Poster

Rabbit
Robe
Roller skates
Rooster
Rubber duck
Run

Sandbox
Saucer
Scarf
Seesaw
Sheep
Shirt
Shoes
Shovel
Sing
Sink
Sister
Skateboard
Skirt
Sleep
Slide
Sneakers
Soap

Socks
Sponge
Spoon
Sweater
Swing

Teapot
Teddy bear
Tennis racquet
Toothbrush
Toothpaste
Towel
Toy box
Toy car
Train
Tree
Truck
Turtle

Walk
Wash
Window
Window shade